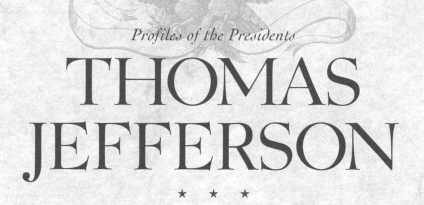

Profiles of the Presidents

THOMAS JEFFERSON

★ ★ ★

Profiles of the Presidents

THOMAS JEFFERSON

by Ann Heinrichs

Content Adviser: Thomas Jefferson Foundation, Charlottesville, Virginia
Social Science Adviser: Professor Sherry L. Field, Department of Curriculum and Instruction, College of Education, The University of Texas at Austin
Reading Adviser: Dr. Linda D. Labbo, Department of Reading Education, College of Education, The University of Georgia

COMPASS POINT BOOKS ✦ MINNEAPOLIS, MINNESOTA

Compass Point Books
3722 West 50th Street, #115
Minneapolis, MN 55410

Visit Compass Point Books on the Internet at *www.compasspointbooks.com*
or e-mail your request to *custserv@compasspointbooks.com*

Photographs ©: White House Collection, courtesy White House Historical Association, cover, 3;
Digital Stock, 6; Burstein Collection/Corbis, 7; Buddy Mays/Corbis, 9, 44, 46, 47, 54 (left), 59
(middle left); Richard T. Nowitz/Corbis, 10; Dave G. Houser/Corbis, 11 (top), 15, 55 (top right);
Stock Montage, 11 (bottom), 35, 39, 54 (right), 58 (left); Bettmann/Corbis, 12, 14, 41, 57 (bottom
left); Digital Vision, 13, 32, 50; Hulton Getty/Archive Photos, 16, 21, 24, 27, 28, 30, 31, 36, 49,
55 (all), 56 (left), 57 (right), 58 (right); North Wind Picture Archives, 18, 19, 20, 23, 29, 34, 42;
Owen Franken/Corbis, 22; Bequest of Mrs. Benjamin Ogle Tayloe, Collection of The Corcoran
Gallery of Art/Corbis, 25; Nancy Carter/North Wind Picture Archives, 37; AP/Wide World Photos,
38; Joseph Sohm, ChromoSohm Inc./Corbis, 48, 59 (bottom left).

Editors: E. Russell Primm, Emily J. Dolbear, and Melissa McDaniel
Photo Researchers: Svetlana Zhurkina and Jo Miller
Photo Selector: Catherine Neitge
Designer: The Design Lab

Library of Congress Cataloging-in-Publication Data

Heinrichs, Ann.
    Thomas Jefferson / by Ann Heinrichs.
      p. cm. — (Profiles of the presidents)
    Includes bibliographical references and index.
    Summary: Discusses the personal life and political career of the author of the Declaration of
Independence, who became the third president of the United States.
    ISBN 0-7565-0206-3 (hardcover)
    1. Jefferson, Thomas, 1743–1826—Juvenile literature. 2. Presidents—United States—Biography—
Juvenile literature. [1. Jefferson, Thomas, 1743–1826. 2. Presidents.] I. Title. II. Series.
E332.79 .H45 2002
    973.4'6'092—dc21   2001004738

© 2002 by Compass Point Books

Printed in the United States of America.

Table of Contents

★ ★ ★

Inventing America

* * *

We hold these truths to be self-evident, that all men are created equal; that they are endowed by their Creator with certain unalienable Rights, that among these are Life, Liberty and the pursuit of Happiness.

A statue of ▶
Thomas Jefferson
stands in the
Jefferson Memorial
in Washington, D.C.
On the walls are
the great words
from the Declaration
of Independence.

Thomas Jefferson is best known for writing these words. Some people say he invented America when he wrote them. As the new nation was struggling to be born, Jefferson put its hopes and dreams into words.

At a time when most nations had kings and queens and national religions,

Jefferson called for a new kind of government. This new government would respect people's freedom—the freedom to think, speak, and act without fear of punishment. This new government would be the servant of the people, not their master. Jefferson's vision became the United States of America. He would serve as the nation's third president.

Today, both Democrats and Republicans claim Jefferson's ideas as their own. He is also a symbol of

▲ *A portrait of Thomas Jefferson by famous American painter Gilbert Stuart*

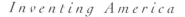

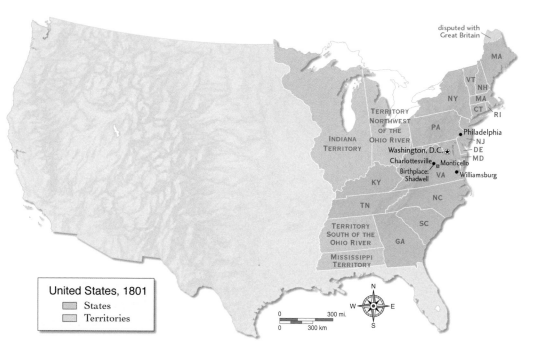

United States, 1801
- States
- Territories

freedom around the world. Wherever people thirst for freedom, they look to Jefferson.

Jefferson gave us a treasure of written material. His work covers politics, religion, science, nature, and many other subjects. Yet Jefferson himself is something of a mystery. His life was filled with contrasts. He stood for the common people, but he lived in **luxury**. He slashed government spending, though he himself was deep in debt. He fought for freedom and **equality** for all, yet he held many slaves. Still, Thomas Jefferson continues to inspire everyone who believes in "Life, Liberty, and the pursuit of Happiness."

The Early Years

★ ★ ★

Thomas Jefferson was born on April 13, 1743. His parents, Peter and Jane Randolph Jefferson, lived on a plantation called Shadwell. It lay in the rolling hills near Charlottesville in the colony of Virginia. To the west, the Jeffersons could see the misty outlines of the Blue Ridge Mountains.

Jane came from a wealthy Virginia family. Peter was a strong, rugged outdoorsman. He often took young Tom with him on his trips through the woods.

◀ Jefferson grew up in the hills near Charlottesville, where he later built his home, Monticello.

9

Peter was well respected in the region. He served as a sheriff, a justice of the peace, and a lieutenant colonel in the Virginia **militia**. He was also a **burgess**—a representative in the Virginia **colony's legislature**.

Tom was a bright young man. When he was very young, he was already reading his father's books. He

began his schooling when he was five years old. At nine, he went to a boarding school in Northam. Soon Tom was able to read Latin and Greek and to play the violin. He was growing, too. When he became a tall, thin teenager, friends called him "Long Tom." He and a friend often rode up to a mountaintop overlooking Charlottesville. "Someday I'll build a house here," Tom would say. They started calling it "Tom's Mountain."

▲ *Thomas Jefferson attended school on the Tuckahoe Plantation near Richmond.*

When Tom was fourteen, his father died. Suddenly, he was the oldest male in his family, with six younger sisters and a baby brother. Still, he kept up with his education. His father had taught him how important it was.

At sixteen, Tom saddled his horse and rode off to Williamsburg, Virginia. There he attended The College of William and Mary.

Tom enjoyed being away at college. He loved playing cards and going to parties and horse races. Then one day he realized that it was time to get serious. He began studying fifteen hours a day. After two years at William and Mary, he was ready to move on. Tom went to study law in the office of George Wythe, the top lawyer in Virginia at that time.

One day in 1765, the young Mr. Jefferson attended a session of the Virginia House of Burgesses. Britain had just passed the Stamp

▲ *Jefferson began his studies at The College of William and Mary when he was sixteen.*

◀ *George Wythe*

Patrick Henry ▶
delivering a fiery
speech

Act. Americans had to pay heavy taxes because of this act. Jefferson heard a burgess named Patrick Henry deliver a fiery speech against Britain's king. In 1768, Jefferson himself was elected to the Virginia **House of Burgesses.**

Meanwhile, Jefferson began drawing plans for his house on "Tom's Mountain." He named the mountaintop

Monticello, meaning "Little Mountain," and built a small brick house there. It would have to do until the big house was ready. Soon he began seeing a young lady named Martha Wayles Skelton. She was lovely and graceful and loved music. The two were married on New Year's Day, 1772, and baby Martha arrived in the fall.

Work continued on Jefferson's big house, and soon the family moved in. Monticello overlooked the 5,000-acre (2,023-hectare) **plantation** Jefferson's father had left him. More than fifty slaves worked in the fields, stables, dairy, blacksmith shop, carpenter shop, and sawmill at Monticello.

◀ *Monticello*

Benjamin Banneker

Black Heritage USA 15c

A postage stamp ▶
honors Benjamin
Banneker.

It's hard to be sure how Jefferson felt about slavery. He introduced several bills in the Virginia legislature to free the slaves, but all were rejected. But he wrote at other times that blacks were not as smart or as talented as whites. Benjamin Banneker, an African-American mathematician, asked Jefferson how he could believe in racial equality and still believe this. Jefferson never answered the question. However, he told Banneker that blacks have "talents equal to those of the other colors of men." He said those talents were not always seen because many blacks were slaves.

In time, Jefferson's neighbors and relatives began freeing their slaves. But Jefferson held on, freeing only a few. He said it would be "like abandoning children" to turn them out into a white world.

Revolutionary Times

★ ★ ★

Jefferson soon had to leave his home and family behind. Like many other people in the American colonies, he was excited about the idea of freedom from Britain. In 1775, the leaders of the colonies decided to hold a Continental Congress in Philadelphia, Pennsylvania. Jefferson was chosen to represent Virginia. By then, the Jeffersons had a second little daughter. Jefferson was sorry to leave his family at such a happy time in his life, but duty called.

◄ Delegates to the First Continental Congress met in Carpenter's Hall in Philadelphia.

A group that ▶
included Benjamin
Franklin, Thomas
Jefferson, John
Adams, Roger
Sherman, and
Robert Livingstone
worked on the
Declaration of
Independence.

In Philadelphia, Jefferson met with many great Americans—Benjamin Franklin, John Adams, and others. They all had heard of Jefferson. Back in Virginia, he had written a booklet explaining why the colonies should be free from Britain. Everyone thought it was brilliant.

After many meetings, Congress decided it was time to declare independence from Britain. The American Revolution had broken out in April 1775, and by now the war was in full swing. Jefferson and John Adams had great respect for each other. Each man thought the other should write the Declaration of Independence. Because Jefferson was such a fine writer, however, the job went to him.

Jefferson worked alone in a rented room. Through the night he worked by candlelight—writing, crossing out, rethinking, and rewriting. Now and then he stopped and played the violin to refresh his mind. At last the declaration was completed. From July 2 to July 4, Congress discussed Jefferson's work and made changes here and there. But only one small change was made before this section was approved:

"We hold these truths to be self-evident; that all men are created equal; that they are endowed by their Creator with certain unalienable rights; that among these are Life,

★

▲ *Jefferson wrote the declaration in his rented room.*

Liberty and the pursuit of Happiness; that to secure these rights, governments are instituted among men, deriving their just powers from the consent of the governed."

Today it is considered the heart of the declaration by many people—and the essence of what Americans believe. On July 4, 1776, Congress adopted the Declaration of Independence. At that moment, the United States of America was born.

Jefferson headed back to Virginia and took his place in the legislature there. Fired up with the ideas of freedom and equality, he began to make sweeping changes. He changed laws so that people's land would be distributed more evenly after they died. He also worked to change the education system. As it was, only wealthy people could get a good education. Jefferson believed that anyone who had the ability deserved an education.

Jefferson also tried to encourage a division between church and government. He felt strongly about religious freedom, too. His "Statute of Virginia for Religious Freedom" was one of his finest works.

Jefferson was elected governor of Virginia in 1779. By that time, the Revolutionary War had reached Virginia,

▲ *A draft of the declaration in Jefferson's handwriting*

An American ▸
soldier

and British troops were spreading all over the region.
Jefferson took his family away for safety. All but two of
the Jeffersons' five children had died when they were very
young, and he did not want to lose any more. But many
Virginians blamed him for leaving and called him a cow-

ard. In 1781, Jefferson's term as governor ended. Tired of public life, he went home to live in peace with his family.

Unfortunately, all was not well at home. His wife, Martha, was very ill after giving birth to their sixth child. One daughter wrote: "He nursed my poor mother, sitting up with her and administering her medicine and drink. For the four months that she lingered, he was never out of calling." Jefferson promised Martha on her deathbed that he would never marry again.

▲ *This engraving of Thomas Jefferson was made in about 1780.*

When Martha died in September 1782, Jefferson fainted and had to be carried to his room. He had already lost three infant children. After so many heartbreaks, he said, "I am born to lose everything I love."

An American in Paris

★ ★ ★

Gradually, Jefferson got back to work. In 1784, Congress asked him to serve as U.S. **minister** to France. He would work out agreements with France and keep up friend-ly relations between the two countries. In July, he and his eleven-year-old daughter, Martha, sailed for France. Later he

This plaque marks the site of Thomas Jefferson's home in Paris during the years he served as minister to France.

brought his daughter Mary to France, too. Sadly, his daughter Lucy died while he was in Paris.

Jefferson was a popular guest in the beautiful capital city of Paris. He enjoyed the city's art, music, and

architecture. Inventions such as matches and pasta-mak-
ing machines fascinated him. He sent books, seeds, and
plants home to Virginia.

▲ *A battle during
the French
Revolution*

French politics excited him, too. France was about to
have a revolution—one that called for "liberty, equality, and
fraternity." The French were ready for **democracy** instead of
kings and queens. Jefferson knew those feelings well.

In spite of the good times, Jefferson was lonely. In
1786, he fell in love with the beautiful Maria Cosway, who
shared his love for music and art. They had delightful times
strolling along the banks of the River Seine and taking
carriage rides into the countryside. But the romance had to
end. Jefferson had promised never to remarry—and Maria

herself was married. Jefferson was torn apart inside. He shared his feelings in a letter to Maria that contained a "Dialogue Between My Head and My Heart."

Jefferson soon learned that the United States had drawn up a **constitution** that spelled out how the country would be governed. He was not sure he liked it, though. It outlined the government's powers, but Jefferson was

The Bill of Rights ▶

more interested in the people's rights. He thought there should be a bill of rights saying what the government could *not* do to its people. Later, in 1791, the first ten amendments, or additions, to the U.S. Constitution became the Bill of Rights. It guaranteed many of Jefferson's favorite ideas, including freedom of speech and separation of church and state.

The United States was forming its first government, with George Washington as president. Washington wrote Jefferson and asked him to come back from France. Washington wanted Jefferson to be the new nation's first secretary of state. With the French Revolution beginning, Jefferson knew it was time to leave. He and his daughters packed up and sailed back to America.

▲ A portrait of George Washington by painter Gilbert Stuart

Party Politics

★ ★ ★

Jefferson had been away for five years. Now he was to
help govern the brand-new United States. At this point,
everything was a big experiment. No one was quite sure
how things should work.

Jefferson took his place among President Washington's
cabinet, or group of advisers. It consisted of only four
men. Jefferson was secretary of state, and Alexander
Hamilton was secretary of the treasury. There was also
a secretary of war and an attorney general. Jefferson's
old friend John Adams was the vice president.

Jefferson and Hamilton fought from the start.
Hamilton believed in a strong national government.
Jefferson thought power belonged with the states and the
people. Hamilton liked to help businessmen and bankers,
while Jefferson favored helping farmers and craftspeople.
Hamilton was friendly toward Britain because it was good

◂ *Members of
Washington's
cabinet included
Henry Knox,
Thomas Jefferson,
Edmund Randolph,
and Alexander
Hamilton.*

Thomas Jefferson and Alexander Hamilton are shown meeting with George Washington in this famous painting by Constantino Brumidi in the Senate reception room at the U.S. Capitol.

for trade. Jefferson liked France because it had gone through a revolution like America's. Both men had many supporters in Congress.

Soon there were two clear camps—Federalists and Republicans. Hamilton's supporters were the Federalists. Jefferson's supporters were the Republicans, later called the Democratic-Republicans. This was the beginning of the nation's political party system.

For people today, this can be confusing. Today's Republican Party was born in 1854. Today's Democratic Party traces its history back to the Democratic-Republican Party of Jefferson's time.

Jefferson and Hamilton continued to lock horns. Finally, Jefferson had had enough. In 1793 he quit his office. "I have no ambition to govern men," he said. "It is a painful and thankless office." He went home, hoping never to be in politics again.

Things did not work out that way, however. George Washington would soon be stepping down after his second term as president. With the Federalists gaining power, the Republicans talked Jefferson into running for president in 1796.

▲ *A statue of Thomas Jefferson at the University of Virginia*

In those days, several people ran for president. Average citizens did not choose the president. Instead, each state appointed electors to represent its people. Each elector voted for one candidate. The person who got the most

John Adams ▲

votes became president. The person who came in second became vice president. In the 1796 election, John Adams came in first. Jefferson, only three votes behind him, would be vice president.

Jefferson had a hard time working under Adams. Adams had become a solid Federalist, and Jefferson often disagreed with him. Their worst quarrel arose over the Alien and Sedition Acts of 1798. These laws made it a crime to speak out against the government.

Jefferson had always believed in the right to hold opposing views. He thought the Alien and Sedition Acts went against the "spirit of '76"—everything Americans had fought for in the revolution.

The 1800 presidential campaign was a brutal battle. Jefferson, Adams, and several others were running. Religious leaders called Jefferson an **atheist** and a devil because he supported freedom of religion. In the end, Jefferson and a Republican named Aaron Burr tied for first place. Adams came in third place.

Now the U.S. House of Representatives had to break the tie. It took them one week. The congressmen brought in their pillows and blankets so they could sleep between votes. After thirty-six votes, Jefferson finally won. He would be the third president of the United States. Aaron Burr, in second place, would be vice president. Jefferson did not really trust Burr, but he had no choice.

▲ *Aaron Burr*

The faces of presidents (from left) George Washington, Thomas Jefferson, Theodore Roosevelt, and Abraham Lincoln adorn Mount Rushmore.

Jefferson called this election a second American Revolution. It was the first time power had moved from one party to another. As rough as the election was, Jefferson was pleased that it had all happened peacefully, according to the Constitution.

The Third President

★ ★ ★

Jefferson began his presidency on a note of friendship.
He gave a speech urging everyone to work together.
"We are all Republicans," he said; "we are all Federalists."
Jefferson's approach was a model for the future. Presidential winners have reached out in friendship to the losers
ever since.

As president, the first thing Jefferson had to do was
put his cabinet together. A loyal friend, James Madison,
was secretary of state. Madison would later be the nation's
fourth president. Albert Gallatin was secretary of the
treasury. He was an excellent money manager and a
strong Republican leader.

Although there were many Federalists in Congress,
Jefferson persuaded everyone to work together. He was
able to lower taxes, cut spending, and get rid of some
government jobs. He did this because he believed that

James Madison ▶

the national government should not be too strong. Power, he believed, belonged with the states.

Jefferson held weekly dinner parties at the White House. His daughter, Martha Jefferson Randolph, often served as his First Lady and White House hostess. Unlike the formal dinners Adams had held, Jefferson's parties were relaxed. People sat at round tables. This meant that all had an equal position of importance. Jefferson was just as relaxed around the house. He welcomed all visitors and often greeted them wearing his house shoes.

▲ *Martha Jefferson Randolph*

The Louisiana Purchase of 1803 was one of Jefferson's greatest achievements as president. The vast Louisiana Territory had belonged to France. The territory stretched from the Mississippi River Valley west to the Rocky Mountains. But France was at war with Britain and needed money. So Jefferson bought the Louisiana Territory for about $15 million. This purchase doubled the size of the United States.

Jefferson had been planning to send out a party to explore the territory. In 1804, his private secretary, Meriwether Lewis, and a man named William Clark set out with the group. Lewis and Clark sent back descriptions of animals, plants, mountains, rivers, and the customs of the native people they met.

Jefferson was a popular president. But he still had enemies, and trouble was brewing for him. In 1802, a

Western artist ▶
Charles Russell
painted this picture
of the Lewis and
Clark expedition.

writer named James Callender began publishing stories
that attacked Jefferson's personal life. Callender had
once worked for Jefferson, writing stories against the
Federalists. He had expected to get a high-paying government job in return. When this did not happen, he turned
against Jefferson.

▲ *Lewis and Clark named the Jefferson River in Montana to honor the president.*

Jefferson admitted one of Callender's charges. He
confessed that, before he was married, he had flirted
improperly with a friend's wife. He said that was the only

Descendants of ▶
Martha Jefferson
and of Sally
Hemings posed
for a group
picture at
Monticello.

truthful charge against him. Callender had also written that Jefferson had a long, close relationship with one of his slaves—Sally Hemings. As a result, he said, Jefferson was the father of Sally's children.

Americans have wondered about this for 200 years. Finally, in the late 1990s, a group of scientists and historians studied the issue. They concluded that Jefferson was most likely the father of Sally's son Eston. They also said that Jefferson was very possibly the father of several of Sally's other children. Other scientists and historians disagree, however. So the debate will probably go on for another 200 years.

The Second Time Around

★ ★ ★

In spite of the stories going around, Jefferson easily won reelection. But his second term as president would be much harder than his first.

Federalists kept attacking Jefferson in the newspapers. They complained about his work as president as well as about his personal life. Jefferson had always believed in freedom of speech and freedom of the press. After all, his own writings had helped create a new nation. Now he

▲ *Thomas Jefferson*

was the victim of free speech. He began to wonder if that kind of freedom was such a good thing after all. Turning against his own beliefs, he had some of his Federalist critics charged with crimes.

Jefferson's former vice president, Aaron Burr, was causing problems, too. Burr led a group into what was then the southwestern United States. To this day, no one knows exactly what he had in mind. It seemed that Burr wanted to break the Southwest off from the rest of the United States and rule it himself. Jefferson was outraged and had Burr arrested for **treason.** There was not enough evidence to prove it, however, so Burr was set free.

Meanwhile, France and Britain were at war again. Both countries blockaded their ports. That meant that any ship that traded with their enemy was not allowed to land. American ships were caught in the middle. Both nations were also stopping American ships.

Jefferson was determined not to take sides. That would only pull the United States into the war. Instead, he passed his own blockade—the Embargo Act of 1807. It stopped all trade between the United States and foreign countries. Jefferson thought this would hurt France and England and force them to change.

◀ *Aaron Burr on trial for treason*

▲ *Goods were moved overland during the embargo.*

As it turned out, America wasn't yet big enough to make much difference to England and France. Instead, the blockade damaged the U.S. economy. It hurt New Englanders, who depended heavily on trade. It also hurt farmers who sold cotton and tobacco to Europe. The once-popular president fell from grace.

In 1808, the next presidential election was approaching. At that time, there was no limit on how many terms a president could scrvc. People began asking Jefferson to run for a third time. The Embargo Act had been a disaster, but many Americans still thought Jefferson was a hero.

Jefferson, however, felt beaten down and tired. He had tried to keep the country out of a war, but his efforts had backfired. He had always admired George Washington for stepping down after two terms. It seemed like a good idea to Jefferson, too. Now he just wanted to go home to

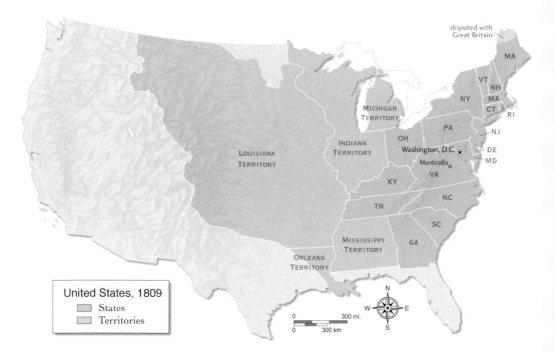

United States, 1809
— States
— Territories

Paintings hang on the wall over the fireplace in the parlor of Monticello.

Monticello. As he looked forward to happy days among his gardens and trees, he wrote, "Never did a prisoner released from his chains feel such relief as I shall in shaking off the shackles of power."

Jefferson Still Lives!

★　★　★

After he retired, Jefferson was busier than ever. At home in Monticello, he filled his days with gardening and rebuilding his house. His daughter Martha was there, and he enjoyed romping and playing with her children. Visitors dropped by constantly, too. Sometimes there were as many as fifty guests at once in his large house.

On a typical day, Jefferson rose before dawn and soaked his feet in cold water. He wrote letters for a few hours, taking a break only for breakfast. Then he would ride on horseback around Monticello and direct the work in his gardens. In the late afternoon, he had dinner with his family and guests. When darkness fell, he settled in the parlor to read. Often his grandchildren sat quietly around him, reading like Grandpa. Around 10:00 P.M. he went to bed.

▲ *Jefferson's reading glasses*

One day in 1812, Jefferson got a letter from his old friend—and enemy—John Adams. Adams thought they should start writing to each other. Jefferson agreed. The two old heroes of the nation's early days became great friends again through their letters.

Jefferson had one last dream—to leave behind a special gift. He founded the University of Virginia at Charlottesville, which was opened in 1825. He chose a beautiful spot for the school. He also designed the university's buildings, planned its classes, and began

choosing the books for its library. This was the nation's first public college—the first that was not founded by a religious group. Today the University of Virginia is one of the top universities in the nation.

A couple walks outside the Rotunda on the University of Virginia campus, which Jefferson designed.

As the end of his life drew near, Jefferson decided what should be written on his tomb. It was to read: "Here was buried Thomas Jefferson: Author of the Declaration of American Independence, of the Statute of Virginia for Religious Freedom, and Father of the University of Virginia." Jefferson was proudest of these three things.

Thomas Jefferson's ▶
tombstone in the
family cemetery at
Monticello

Even being president was not as important to him.

Both Jefferson and Adams were looking forward to July 4, 1826. That would be the fiftieth anniversary of the Declaration of Independence. They were proud of the nation that had been born under their care. As the big day approached, both men were very ill. But they both seemed determined to live to see the Fourth of July.

On the night of July 3, Jefferson was barely alive. But he kept waking and asking, "Is it the Fourth?" After midnight, someone finally answered yes. Jefferson never spoke again. He died on July 4 at about 12:50 in the afternoon. At the same time, his old friend John Adams lay on his deathbed, too. Around 5:00 P.M., Adams cried, "Thomas Jefferson still

▲ *Thomas Jefferson*

lives!" He had not yet learned of Jefferson's death, and the thought of his old friend filled him with joy. Then he, too, died.

In a way, Adams was right when he spoke his final words. Thomas Jefferson still lives in the minds and hearts of freedom lovers everywhere. He lives wherever people yearn for "Life, Liberty, and the pursuit of Happiness."

The Thomas Jefferson Memorial in Washington, D.C.

GLOSSARY

★ ★ ★

atheist—someone who does not believe in God

burgess—a member of the colonial legislature of either Virginia or Maryland

cabinet—a president's group of advisers

colony—a territory settled by people from another country and ruled by that country

constitution—a document stating the basic rules of a government

democracy—a government in which the people elect the leaders

equality—the same rights for everyone

fraternity—a group of people with a common interest; like brothers

House of Burgesses—the legislature of the Virginia colony

legislature—the part of government that makes or changes laws

luxury—an abundance of comfort and wealth

militia—an army of part-time soldiers

minister—an official who represents one country in another country

plantation—a large farm

treason—an attempt to betray one's own country

THOMAS JEFFERSON'S LIFE AT A GLANCE

★ ★ ★

PERSONAL

Nickname: Man of the People

Birth date: April 13, 1743

Birthplace: Shadwell, Virginia

Father's name: Peter Jefferson

Mother's name: Jane Randolph Jefferson

Education: College of William and Mary (1762)

Wife's name: Martha Wayles Skelton

Married: January 1, 1772

Children: Martha Jefferson (1772–1836), Jane Randolph Jefferson (1774–1775), infant son (1777), Mary Jefferson (1778–1804), Lucy Elizabeth Jefferson (1780–1781), Lucy Elizabeth Jefferson (1782–1785)

Death date: July 4, 1826

Place of death: Monticello

Buried: Monticello

PUBLIC

Occupation before presidency:	Lawyer, plantation owner, architect, diplomat
Occupation after presidency:	Plantation owner
Military service:	None
Other government positions:	Member of Virginia House of Burgesses, 1769–1774; member of Continental Congress, 1775–1776; governor of Virginia, 1779–1781; member of Continental Congress, 1783–1785; minister to France, 1785–1789; secretary of state, 1790–1793; vice president, 1797–1801
Political party:	Democratic-Republican
Vice presidents:	Aaron Burr (1801–1805), George Clinton (1805–1809)
Dates in office:	March 4, 1801–March 3, 1809
Presidential opponents:	President John Adams (Federalist), Aaron Burr (Republican), 1800; Charles C. Pinckney (Federalist, 1804)
Number of votes (Electoral College):	73 of 138 in 1800 and 162 of 176 in 1804
Writings:	A Summary View of the Rights of British America (1774); Declaration of Independence (1776); Notes on the State of Virginia (1781–1782); A Manual of Parliamentary Practice for the use of the Senate of the United States (1801)

★

Thomas Jefferson's Cabinet

Secretary of state:
James Madison
(1801–1809)

Secretary of the treasury:
Samuel Dexter
(1801),
Albert Gallatin
(1801–1809)

Secretary of war:
Henry Dearborn
(1801–1809)

Attorney general:
Levi Lincoln
(1801–1804),
John Breckinridge
(1805–1806),
Caesar A. Rodney
(1807–1809)

Secretary of the navy:
Benjamin Stoddert
(1801),
Robert Smith
(1801–1809)

THOMAS JEFFERSON'S LIFE AND TIMES

★ ★ ★

JEFFERSON'S LIFE

April 13, Jefferson is born at Shadwell, Virginia, in the hills where he later built Monticello (below)

1743

WORLD EVENTS

1749   German writer Johann Wolfgang Goethe is born

1750

1752   Benjamin Franklin performs his famous kite experiment (below)

1759   Author Voltaire of France writes his brilliant tale *Candide*

The British Museum opens in London

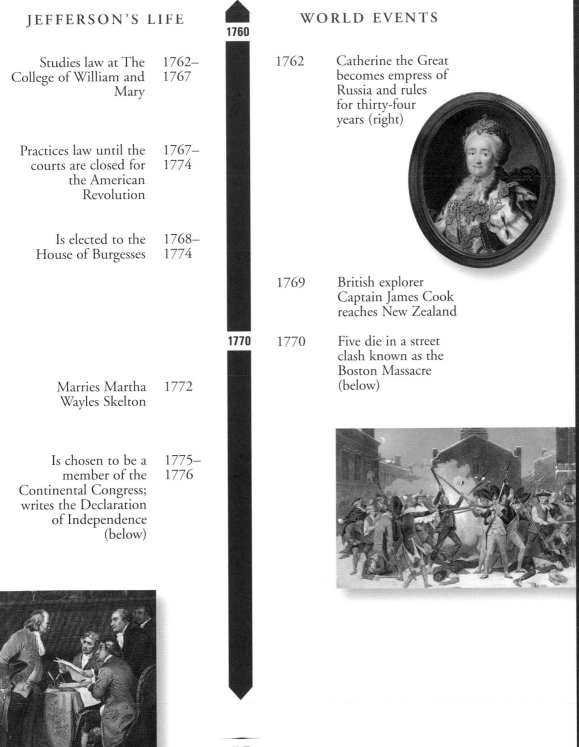

JEFFERSON'S LIFE

Studies law at The College of William and Mary — 1762–1767

Practices law until the courts are closed for the American Revolution — 1767–1774

Is elected to the House of Burgesses — 1768–1774

Marries Martha Wayles Skelton — 1772

Is chosen to be a member of the Continental Congress; writes the Declaration of Independence (below) — 1775–1776

1760

1770

WORLD EVENTS

1762 — Catherine the Great becomes empress of Russia and rules for thirty-four years (right)

1769 — British explorer Captain James Cook reaches New Zealand

1770 — Five die in a street clash known as the Boston Massacre (below)

JEFFERSON'S LIFE		WORLD EVENTS	
Serves in the Virginia legislature	1776–1779	1777	Vermont is the first former colony to ban slavery
Serves as governor of Virginia	1779–1781	1779	Jan Ingenhousz of the Netherlands discovers that plants release oxygen when exposed to sunlight
	1780		
Serves in the Continental Congress	1783–1784	1783	American author Washington Irving is born
Serves as minister to France	1784–1789		
Serves as secretary of state	1790–1793	**1790**	
		1791	Austrian composer Wolfgang Amadeus Mozart dies
Is elected vice president under John Adams	1796		
		1799	Napoléon Bonaparte (left) takes control of France
			The Rosetta stone, which was the key to understanding Egyptian hieroglyphics, was found near Rosetta, Egypt

★

JEFFERSON'S LIFE

1800

1801 The Supreme Court decides *Marbury v. Madison,* defining the role of the Supreme Court and its ability to declare laws unconstitutional

1803 Louisiana Territory is purchased from France; Ohio joins the Union

Meriwether Lewis and William Clark are sent to explore the Louisiana Territory (below)

Aaron Burr kills Alexander Hamilton in a duel (right)

WORLD EVENTS

1801 Ultraviolet radiation is discovered

United States, 1809
States
Territories

Presidential Election Results:		Popular Votes	Electoral Votes
1800	Thomas Jefferson	Not Available	73
	Aaron Burr		73
1804	Thomas Jefferson	Not Available	162
	Charles C. Pinckney		14

JEFFERSON'S LIFE

1807 Hosts with his daughter, Martha Randolph (below), the first inaugural open house and begins the tradition of opening the White House for annual receptions on New Year's Day and the Fourth of July. The custom continued until the 1930s.

The U.S. ship *Chesapeake* is attacked by the British ship *Leopard,* almost bringing the United States and Britain to war

WORLD EVENTS

1805 General anesthesia is first used in surgery

1807 Robert Fulton's *Clermont* (below) is the first reliable steamship to travel between New York City and Albany

1810 Bernardo O'Higgins (above) leads Chile in its fight for independence from Spain

1810

JEFFERSON'S LIFE

Resumes correspon- 1812
dence with old friend
John Adams

The University of 1825
Virginia (above),
founded by
Jefferson, opens

July 4, dies and is 1826
buried (below) at
Monticello

WORLD EVENTS

1812– The United States
1814 and Britain fight the
War of 1812

1814– European states
1815 meet in Vienna,
Austria, to redraw
national borders after
the conclusion of the
Napoleonic Wars

1820

1820 Susan B. Anthony,
a leader of the
American woman
suffrage movement,
is born

1823 Mexico becomes
a republic

1826 The first photograph
is taken by Joseph
Niépce, a French
physicist

UNDERSTANDING THOMAS JEFFERSON AND HIS PRESIDENCY

★ ★ ★

IN THE LIBRARY

Jones, Veda Boyd; Arthur M. Schlesinger, ed. *Thomas Jefferson: Author of the Declaration of Independence.* Broomall, Penn.: Chelsea House, 2000.

Meltzer, Milton. *Thomas Jefferson: The Revolutionary Aristocrat.* New York: Franklin Watts, 1991.

Severance, John B. *Thomas Jefferson: Architect of Democracy.* New York: Houghton Mifflin, 1998.

ON THE WEB

Monticello—Home of Thomas Jefferson
http://www.monticello.org
For links and information about Jefferson's home

The Letters of Thomas Jefferson: 1743–1826
http://odur.let.rug.nl/~usa/P/tj3/writings/brf/jeflxx.htm
For Thomas Jefferson's letters, arranged by date and by recipient

Ken Burns's PBS film about Thomas Jefferson
http://www.pbs.org/jefferson/
To explore archives, learn about the making of the film, and other information

Understanding Thomas Jefferson
and His Presidency

Thomas Jefferson on Politics and Government
http://etext.virginia.edu/jefferson/quotations/
For quotations from the writings of the president

JEFFERSON HISTORIC SITES
ACROSS THE COUNTRY

**Jefferson National
Expansion Memorial**
11 North Fourth Street
St. Louis, MO 63102
314/655-1700
To visit the Gateway Arch, the
Museum of Westward Expansion,
and St. Louis's Old Courthouse

**Lewis and Clark
National Historic Trail**
1709 Jackson Street
Omaha, NE 68102
402/514-9311
To follow in the westward
footsteps of Lewis and Clark

**Lewis and Clark
Interpretive Center**
P.O. Box 1806
Great Falls, MT 59403
406/727-8733
To attend exhibits and lectures
relating to the travels of Lewis
and Clark

**Monticello Historic Site—
Home of Thomas Jefferson**
Thomas Jefferson Parkway
(Route 53)
Charlottesville, VA 22902
434/984-9822
To tour Jefferson's home; on the
World Heritage list of sites

**Thomas Jefferson
Memorial**
900 Ohio Drive, S.W.
Washington, DC 20024-2000
202/426-6841
To view the tribute to
Jefferson's life and legacy

THE U.S. PRESIDENTS
(Years in Office)

★ ★ ★

1. **George Washington**
   (March 4, 1789-March 3, 1797)
2. **John Adams**
   (March 4, 1797-March 3, 1801)
3. **Thomas Jefferson**
   (March 4, 1801-March 3, 1809)
4. **James Madison**
   (March 4, 1809-March 3, 1817)
5. **James Monroe**
   (March 4, 1817-March 3, 1825)
6. **John Quincy Adams**
   (March 4, 1825-March 3, 1829)
7. **Andrew Jackson**
   (March 4, 1829-March 3, 1837)
8. **Martin Van Buren**
   (March 4, 1837-March 3, 1841)
9. **William Henry Harrison**
   (March 6, 1841-April 4, 1841)
10. **John Tyler**
    (April 6, 1841-March 3, 1845)
11. **James K. Polk**
    (March 4, 1845-March 3, 1849)
12. **Zachary Taylor**
    (March 5, 1849-July 9, 1850)
13. **Millard Fillmore**
    (July 10, 1850-March 3, 1853)
14. **Franklin Pierce**
    (March 4, 1853-March 3, 1857)
15. **James Buchanan**
    (March 4, 1857-March 3, 1861)
16. **Abraham Lincoln**
    (March 4, 1861-April 15, 1865)
17. **Andrew Johnson**
    (April 15, 1865-March 3, 1869)

18. **Ulysses S. Grant**
    (March 4, 1869-March 3, 1877)
19. **Rutherford B. Hayes**
    (March 4, 1877-March 3, 1881)
20. **James Garfield**
    (March 4, 1881-Sept 19, 1881)
21. **Chester Arthur**
    (Sept 20, 1881-March 3, 1885)
22. **Grover Cleveland**
    (March 4, 1885-March 3, 1889)
23. **Benjamin Harrison**
    (March 4, 1889-March 3, 1893)
24. **Grover Cleveland**
    (March 4, 1893-March 3, 1897)
25. **William McKinley**
    (March 4, 1897-
    September 14, 1901)
26. **Theodore Roosevelt**
    (September 14, 1901-
    March 3, 1909)
27. **William Howard Taft**
    (March 4, 1909-March 3, 1913)
28. **Woodrow Wilson**
    (March 4, 1913-March 3, 1921)
29. **Warren G. Harding**
    (March 4, 1921-August 2, 1923)
30. **Calvin Coolidge**
    (August 3, 1923-March 3, 1929)
31. **Herbert Hoover**
    (March 4, 1929-March 3, 1933)
32. **Franklin D. Roosevelt**
    (March 4, 1933-April 12, 1945)

33. **Harry S. Truman**
    (April 12, 1945-
    January 20, 1953)
34. **Dwight D. Eisenhower**
    (January 20, 1953-
    January 20, 1961)
35. **John F. Kennedy**
    (January 20, 1961-
    November 22, 1963)
36. **Lyndon B. Johnson**
    (November 22, 1963-
    January 20, 1969)
37. **Richard M. Nixon**
    (January 20, 1969-
    August 9, 1974)
38. **Gerald R. Ford**
    (August 9, 1974-
    January 20, 1977)
39. **James Earl Carter**
    (January 20, 1977-
    January 20, 1981)
40. **Ronald Reagan**
    (January 20, 1981-
    January 20, 1989)
41. **George H. W. Bush**
    (January 20, 1989-
    January 20, 1993)
42. **William Jefferson Clinton**
    (January 20, 1993-
    January 20, 2001)
43. **George W. Bush**
    (January 20, 2001-)

INDEX

★ ★ ★

ABOUT THE AUTHOR

Ann Heinrichs grew up in Fort Smith, Arkansas. She began playing the piano at age three and thought she would grow up to be a pianist. Instead, she became a writer. Now she has written more than fifty books for children and young adults. Several of her books have won national awards. Ms. Heinrichs now lives in Chicago, Illinois. She enjoys martial arts and traveling to faraway countries.

DATE DUE

MAY 1 7 2010